Original title:
Sunset on the Horizon

Copyright © 2025 Creative Arts Management OÜ
All rights reserved.

Author: Evelyn Hartman
ISBN HARDBACK: 978-1-80581-476-4
ISBN PAPERBACK: 978-1-80581-003-2
ISBN EBOOK: 978-1-80581-476-4

A Dance of Dusk

As the sun dips down, it starts to prance,
Clouds wear their shades, ready to dance.
Birds grumble, 'Hey, we need a break!'
While squirrels snicker, 'For goodness' sake!'

Light twirls around in a silly show,
Casting shadows long, like a giant's toe.
The grass seems to giggle, waving its head,
While the trees whisper jokes, 'It's time for bed!'

Daylight's Endearing Kiss

The day leans in with a toothy grin,
Chasing away the light, oh where to begin?
The sky blushes pink, much to its surprise,
As night pulls a snack from its bag of pies.

Chirps fill the air, a celebratory cheer,
'Pajamas or wine? Let's pick a career!'
With a wink and a nod, the moon takes the stage,
While stars juggle light, a comedic rage!

Horizon's Honeyed Glow

Golden rays spill like syrupy delight,
The world chuckles softly, 'What a sight!'
Cats leap for shadows, while dogs chase light,
As rabbits hop home for their dinner bite.

Colors sprinkle the canvas, a painter's best trick,
'Time to glow up!' they all say, with a flick.
Breezes nudge flowers to join in the fun,
Laughing at day, 'Oh, it's not yet done!'

Twilight's Embrace

The coffee's cooled, the skies turn pink,
As day bids night, we laugh and wink.
My cat's on guard, the shadows creep,
She pounces at ghosts, then falls asleep.

With crayons out, we paint the air,
The world's a mess, we just don't care.
The sun slides down, a perfect prank,
The light plays tricks, and we just tank!

A Palette of Dusk

The sky's a canvas, splashed with glee,
My crayons broke, it's hard to see.
A squirrel flips and dances along,
Calls out to us with a silly song.

The lemonade stands are packing in,
We chat with shadows, let the fun begin.
Bugs all gather for a twilight show,
I swat at them, and hear their woe.

Where Light Meets Darkness

Nighttime's creeping, so here we go,
With pizza slices, and cheesy flow.
We race the dusk on our bikes too fast,
But laughter echoes, it's a blast!

A firefly blinks, a friend in flight,
We're making clumsy plans tonight.
In shadows deep, we chase our dreams,
While tripping over garden themes.

The Last Kiss of Day

As daylight waves its funny hello,
My shadow tricks me, steals the show.
Dancing with birds, I kick up dust,
Pretending I'm a pro, it's a must!

The last light tickles the trees with gold,
While my goofy stories begin to unfold.
The moon peeks in, gives me a nudge,
And giggles as I stumble and budge.

Whispers of the Closing Day

The sky giggles in hues of warm gold,
As if the clouds are getting bold.
A riddle in colors, they twist and dance,
Winking at stars, it's a cosmic romance.

The birds are staging their nightly retreat,
Chasing shadows, they can't be beat.
With flapping wings they pretend to race,
Forget the day, it's a game of space.

A Passage to Nightfall

The sun wears shades, looking quite fly,
On a lazy wave, it's drifting by.
The moon rolls in, cracking a joke,
While crickets join in, ready to croak.

A squirrel watches, munching on a seed,
"Oh twilight dreams, you're exactly what I need!"
Chasing the light, he's late for the show,
Tip-toeing home, he moves way too slow.

Ember's End

The day flickers out like a candle's flame,
But the fireflies come, playing their game.
They twirl in the dusk, like a silly ballet,
While echoes of laughter fill up the gray.

A dog yawns wide, taking a seat,
With a sigh of relief, it's time for a treat.
In the land of z's, he'll snore quite hearty,
Dreaming of bones at the night-time party.

The Paintbrush of Twilight

A bold brush strokes the sky with a grin,
As day says goodbye, let the chaos begin!
Pinks and purples, they clash and collide,
Nature laughs softly, with nothing to hide.

The stars peek out, shy but amused,
At the antics of night, utterly confused.
"Is it time to sparkle?" they nervously blink,
As the evening giggles and winks without a sink.

The Evening's Glow

The sky wears gold like a grand old fool,
Waving goodbye to the sun, doing a cool rule.
Clouds gossip in hues, pinks and oranges bright,
While birds giggle, plotting to stay out late tonight.

A cat stretches wide, claiming the fence,
With a meow that defies all common sense.
Neighbors laugh as the shadows grow long,
Time for a dance to the crickets' song.

Shadows Dance at Dusk

Shadows leap like children playing tag,
Under the streetlamp, a plastic bag.
The moon rolls its eyes at the sun's last show,
As twilight gives way to, well, who knows?

Squirrels throw acorns like party confetti,
While the porch lights flicker: is that a spaghetti?
Neighbors swap tales of their day's grand tricks,
Under the cover of the sky's twilight mix.

Radiance in Retreat

Balloons bob in the breeze like happy little brains,
While the world wraps up in silly refrains.
Fireflies dance in coats of buzzing delight,
Searching for snacks in the next garden fight.

The last sip of lemonade goes down with a splash,
As kids make a mad dash, oh, what a clash!
The sun bows out with a wink and a grin,
Leaving just enough mischief to stir some din.

Crimson Skies Above

A canvas of red with splashes of cream,
As frogs serenade the night with a dream.
Jokes float through the air, oh what a delight,
While stars giggle gently, breaking the night.

The clouds puff up like marshmallows in flight,
Hiding secrets of the day from the night.
Time for silly stories, a raucous debate,
As everyone here celebrates fate's funny traits.

The Last Glimpse of Day

The sky blushes red, what a peculiar sight,
A cow jumps the fence, thinking it's night.
Birds are confused, they chirp with delight,
While squirrels play tag, in their furry flight.

The grass wears a glow from the sun's fading light,
Mice start their dance, oh what a weird sight!
A cat yawns so wide, it dreams of a bite,
As shadows grow longer, the laughter takes flight.

Twilight's Whisper

The day takes a bow, it slips behind trees,
A goat steals my sandwich, with perfect ease.
Clouds wear pajamas, swaying like breeze,
While crickets tune up, to serenade bees.

Bunnies hop in, with whimsy and flair,
Underneath moonlight, they frolic and stare.
I trip on a root, oh how life can be rare,
With twilight above, and mischief in the air.

When Day Meets Night

The sun winks goodbye, just causing a scene,
A raccoon drops pizza, I can't intervene.
Chasing shadows now, like they're part of a team,
The sky wears a hat, purple, pink, and cream.

Fireflies peek out, like stars at a ball,
My puppy insists on chasing them all.
As darkness arrives, we hear night's call,
I laugh at the sight, oh what a free-for-all!

A Canvas of Dimming Gold

Artists paint skies, with all shades and hues,
A squirrel critiques, with its little muse.
The sun drops its brush, to take off its shoes,
While frogs in chorus, sing out their blues.

As colors collide, they giggle and jive,
The willows are dancing, so happy and thrive.
A racquetball rolls, I can't quite describe,
The joy in these moments, where laughter's alive.

Glories of the Evening Sky

A duck in shades, so cool and spry,
With a quack so loud, it makes me cry.
The clouds paint faces, I swear they grin,
As daylight fades, let the laughter begin.

The sun sips tea, then takes a dip,
On clouds like cotton, it starts to flip.
Laughter echoes from the playful breeze,
The sky wears jammies, and it's sure to tease.

Stars peek out, wearing cute little hats,
While crickets dance like tiny acrobats.
The moon winks slyly, a joker at play,
As the day waves goodbye, in a comical way.

A Serenade in Shadows

In the corner, shadows start to prance,
They twirl and spin, in a silly dance.
The sun sneezes gold, with a dramatic flair,
While the trees chuckle, who knows what's there?

A cat bows down, in a formal style,
Chasing her tail, with a giggling smile.
The sky throws confetti, all orange and pink,
As the light fades out, making all of us think.

Fireflies sparkle in a blurry line,
They buzz to the tune of a wrinkly vine.
The laughter grows as the stars come alive,
In this wacky world, the oddest things thrive.

Twilight's Lament

The twilight hums a silly song,
As the critters gather, humming along.
A rabbit wears glasses, reading the news,
While a wise old owl looks puzzled, confused.

The moon throws a party, in its silver glow,
With critters and laughter in a fun show.
The sun packs up, in a bright-colored coat,
And the stars laugh softly, on their tiny boat.

The shadows stretch out, in a goofy slide,
As the warm hues swirl, with nowhere to hide.
With each fading tick, the night starts to joke,
In this twilight dance, a cheerful folk pokes.

The Final Flaming Sigh

The sky takes a bow, in a flamboyant hue,
With flamingo colors, that just can't be true.
A fish on a line, flies up in delight,
Telling the sun, 'This show is just right!'

Down by the pond, a frog sings a tune,
To the winking stars and the lazy moon.
The breeze prances by, kicking up dust,
As the clouds giggle, they know they must trust.

The sun croaks softly, 'Can I stay just one more?'
But the night gives a chuckle, 'There's fun to explore.'
With a wink and a grin, the night takes its stand,
As the day gives a bow, with a wave of its hand.

Constellations in the Making

As the sky paints a cheeky grin,
The stars play tag, who'll win?
A creative spark in the twilight,
Why can't they just sit tight?

A sunbeam winks, slips out of sight,
The moon says, 'I'm the new highlight!'
Giggles echo through the sky,
'Nocturnal fun,' the clouds reply!

The birds bid jokes, fly in a swirl,
Chasing dreams in a feathered whirl.
In the canvas of day's goodbye,
The night's punchline draws nigh.

So let the universe crack a smile,
As laughter travels mile by mile.
With each twinkle, the mischief grows,
In this joke-telling celestial show!

The Day's Last Breath

As daylight wraps in a fuzzy quilt,
The sun retires, not a soul is built.
'Is that a carrot?' asks the moon,
While crickets start their merry tune.

The clouds giggle, puff like cream,
'Night's our party, let's start the dream!'
Shadows stretch, playing peek-a-boo,
They're all ready for their nightly cue!

A remote day shifts to comedy,
Where daylight fades with such glee.
Watch it pass with a dramatic sigh,
The stars roll in, 'Oh my, oh my!'

In this wild dance of time's plight,
The evening claims the jester's right.
So wave goodbye to the sun's good cheer,
And welcome the laughter of night, my dear!

Sultry Twilight Chronicles

The sky blushes, oh what a tease,
While fireflies sip their evening teas.
'Is this glow my new summer dress?'
Says Violet, the haze, in a sparkly mess.

Chasing shadows, they bump and jive,
While echoing laughter keeps dreams alive.
Why did the day wear shades on its face?
'With a glare like mine, it's just common grace!'

Sizzling hues with a wink and a nod,
The breeze swoops in, like a playful prod.
Dance with the night, so lush and round,
In this carnival where joy is found!

A giddy hum fills the pastel air,
'Is it too late for a sunset fair?'
As giggles burst in twilight's glow,
The party of dusk puts on a show!

Horizons of Serenity

As the day waves a goofy goodbye,
A lazy cloud grins as it floats by.
'What's on the menu for tonight's feast?'
'Zzz, just moonbeams, to say the least!'

The sea winks at the sun's retreat,
While sand giggles at dancing feet.
Stars spawn haikus in silent cheer,
While time wraps everyone in a cozy sphere.

On the cusp of dusk, dreams take flight,
Each moment's a prank in this fading light.
'Why are we here?' a starlet may muse,
To spill laughter, in the skies we'll cruise!

With crickets and chirps, take a bow,
A lively show, let's take a vow.
In horizons of peaceful delight,
Find mischief nestled deep in the night!

Where Light Meets Oblivion

The sun slips down, a clumsy clown,
As day gives way, it can't find a gown.
Colors dance like socks on a line,
Who knew twilight could be so divine?

Pinks and yellows, they start to jive,
While nighttime whispers, "I'm still alive!"
A cat yawns wide with a lazy stretch,
Dreaming of fish, oh what a sketch!

Horizon's Soft Farewell

The sky turns peach, like cotton candy,
A seagull quips, "Life is quite dandy!"
Clouds make shapes like a wobbly chair,
There's a sunset party in the open air.

Fishes in ponds start to giggle and splash,
While crickets tap dance, oh what a clash!
I can't help but wonder where all ran off,
Did they leave me behind? Oh, such a scoff!

Luminous Farewell

A bright orb dips like a tumbler's glide,
Painting the world with its golden pride.
Jokes on the clouds, they're too puffy to hide,
It's a balloon celebration; let's take a ride!

Squirrels plot mischief, their fur all aglow,
While fireflies twinkle, putting on a show.
With stars on the rise, what a silly sight,
The universe laughs at the fading light!

The Silence of Dimming Skies

The day yawns loud, then whispers a plea,
"Let's play hide and seek, just you and me!"
As shadows stretch, they trip on their shoes,
Even the moon shares a chuckle or two.

The clouds wear pajamas, all cozy and tight,
As stars pop out, ready for night flight.
A raccoon peeks out, with a grin on his face,
"Who knew the evening could be such a race?"

Hues of Hibernation

As daylight fades, the colors dance,
The sky's a painter, taking a chance.
The clouds giggle, wearing pink and blue,
While the sun slips down, saying, 'Adieu!'

A squirrel sighs in a cozy nook,
Watching the sky, he writes a book.
'Then the night came for a jolly spree,
Wearing stars like shoes, oh so fancy!'

The rabbits hop, making quite a scene,
Chasing the shadows, feeling so keen.
Their laughter echoes as they prance about,
While the moon grins wide, there's never a doubt.

So, gather your friends for this event,
Nature's a joker, laugh till you're bent.
As colors blend in a playful fight,
We bid farewell to the day, with delight.

A Twilight Reverie

The sky blinks twice, time for a show,
Clouds in capes, ready to go.
Daylight sips from its last cup,
While fireflies giggle, lighting up!

Fluffy sheep clouds race as they play,
Whispering secrets of the day:
'Why can't sunsets join in the fun?'
As they blush, losing their golden run.

The trees shimmy to a crickets' beat,
While light starts sneaking, off of its feet.
The stars arrive, wearing silly grins,
At the party where the moon begins!

So bring your snacks, we'll dance till dusk,
In this twilight realm, it's a must!
With jokes and jests that twinkle and shine,
We'll hold onto laughter, one last time.

Night's Gentle Arrival

As daylight dozes, it yawns and sighs,
The moon pops up, in a cheerful guise.
Stars wink like chums who've just come out,
Ready to play, without a doubt.

A boisterous breeze gives the trees a tease,
While shadows stretch, as if saying, 'Please!'
The owls hoot jokes from their lofty heights,
While the bats zoom by in whimsical flights.

A fox plays tricks, twirling 'round and 'round,
While the sun dips low, without a sound.
The night's a canvas, all colors a-fade,
Painting giggles that never degrade.

As laughter spills into the velvety dark,
With creatures stirring, ready to embark.
Let's toast to twilight, with punchlines bright,
In this whimsical world where all's just right.

The Vibrant Goodbye

When the day flips its curtain, oh what a sight,
Colors glisten, bringing sheer delight.
The sky throws a party, with hues gone wild,
Even the sun grins, feeling quite riled.

Golds and purples swirl and collide,
While birds in a frenzy take joyride.
The last of the warmth gives a chuckle and waves,
As shadows make faces in an endearing daze.

The world spins fast, in a playful haste,
While giggling petals dance, no time to waste.
It's a farewell bash where the stars come alive,
Bringing mischief and fun, under moonlight they thrive.

So let's raise a toast to this vibrant goodbye,
With stories and laughter, let's reach for the sky.
As night settles in with a wink and a grin,
We'll carry the joy that the day's light will spin.

Dimming Dazzle

The sky's a painter, oh so bold,
Mixing orange with hints of gold.
Clouds giggle as they drift along,
Even the birds join in the song.

The sun winks down, a playful tease,
While squirrels scurry, gathering leaves.
Nature's disco, with twinkling light,
Shouting 'party' 'til it's night.

Where Colors Bow

Colors bow, take a little bow,
As the day whispers, 'What's up now?'
Pink and purple dance in the air,
While ducks quack stories without a care.

The shadows stretch, a bit too grand,
As ants march home, in a marching band.
It's the twilight's hilarious show,
With laughs all round, an evening glow.

A Farewell in Color

Goodbye to gold, or so they say,
The sun's got jokes before it plays.
Mischief in light, it flickers and fades,
While crickets tune their serenades.

The sky's like a joke, a tricky riddle,
Where twilight tickles the heart a little.
Laughter bounces off the fading beams,
Dreaming of chocolate and silly dreams.

The Serenade of Evening

Evening comes with a cheeky grin,
As fireflies start the dance within.
The world hums a quirky tune,
While stars yawn and play the buffoon.

The moon peeks out, a silver sprite,
Cracking jokes as it takes flight.
With every laugh, the dusk gets bright,
As nature's giggles fill the night.

A Palette of Nightfall

The sky dons a quirky coat,
With orange socks and a purple boat.
Clouds giggle, drifting in delight,
While birds forget their evening flight.

A squirrel, dressed as a captain keen,
Steers a ship of twinkling green.
Stars pop like popcorn in the air,
Laughing at shadows without a care.

The sun waves goodbye with a wink,
As daydreams mingle and thoughts link.
What's for dinner? The moon just shrugs,
While fireflies dance in tiny slugs.

A canvas smeared with laughter bright,
Painting the world in playful light.
In this realm where giggles reign,
Each hue teases the sleepy lane.

Celestial Transitions

The day drops its pants, what a sight,
As colors swirl, oh what delight!
Crickets chirp their nightly tunes,
While the moon flirts with shooting balloons.

The stars poke fun, 'Hey, where'd you go?'
As shadows tickle the evening glow.
A cat plays chess with the fading sun,
While moths debate who's the daring one.

While dusk pulls out its silly cap,
And wraps the world in a gentle nap,
Clouds create mustaches with flair,
As laughter fills the cooling air.

Catch the colors before they blend,
Join the party, no need to pretend.
In this magical, funny-flight,
Every moment sparkles with delight.

The Twilight Context

As colors clash, what a brawl,
The sky yells, 'Catch me, if you can, y'all!'
Cats parade in tuxedos bold,
While trees drop leaves of shimmering gold.

The sun pulls faces, a real show-off,
While clouds do the tango, a funny scoff.
A bench holds secrets of old and new,
Whispering tales simply for you.

The horizon giggles, it can't help but tease,
As fireflies buzz like busy bees.
The sky runs a marathon, oh what a race,
With goofy grins lighting up its face.

Each shade plays tricks, a capricious spree,
In a world where humor floats so free.
Join the mirth as day bids adieu,
Painting the world in its wacky hue.

Softening of the Skies

As the day wears its pajamas tight,
The clouds stock up on shades of bright.
Dandelions giggle in the breeze,
While squirrels play tag with the trees.

The sun paints jokes on a canvas wide,
While the moon rolls in for a nightly ride.
A kitten's yawn echoes far and near,
As crickets cheer with evening cheer.

Stars take the stage with sparkly flair,
In a cosmic dance without a care.
Each twinkle whispers, "What's a fuss?"
While the night wraps the world in a plus.

The atmosphere brings laughter unplanned,
In colors stretching like a rubber band.
So find your giggle as day turns to night,
In this fading laugh of blooming light.

Daybreak's Silent Lullaby

The sun yawns wide, it starts to rise,
Chasing sleep from the distant skies.
Clouds wear pajamas, oh so bright,
Even the birds snore in delight.

Waking up the sleepy town,
Pigeons tumble, and then fall down.
Squirrels stretch like they just awoke,
Laughing at the sleepy oak.

The shadows play tag, just for fun,
Hiding behind every nearby bun.
A rabbit hops, making its run,
Saying to itself, "Time to stun!"

Finally, everyone sings with glee,
Oh day, please be merry, let us see!
As giggles rise from the brink of day,
The sun holds court in its sunny way.

The Evening's Warm Glow

The skies are blushing, feeling shy,
The sun winks, saying goodbye.
Butterflies dance, having a ball,
While crickets prepare for their night call.

The children laugh, their playtime done,
Chasing fireflies, oh what fun!
Mom shouts, "It's time to head home!"
But they just giggle and roam.

The dog rolls over to catch his breath,
His sunset nap, feeling like a feast.
Cats all yawn, in a lazy haze,
Plotting their mischief for the next phase.

As day hands night the golden crown,
The whole world stumbles in a joyful frown.
Painting memories with colors so bright,
Who knew endings could feel so light?

Fading Whispers of a Dying Light

As daylight dims, the shadows blend,
A squirrel slips, oh what a trend!
The sun gives a giggle, slipping away,
While gophers boast at the end of play.

A brave little bug rides on a breeze,
"Catch me if you can!" it teases trees.
But the flowers bow down, too slow to move,
It's the moment they all find their groove.

An owl hoots, it's time for a laugh,
"Hold my acorns, I need a nap!"
Bats take flight with a twist and a shout,
Darkness giggles, casting doubt.

The colors fade, but spirits stay high,
As the stars peek, shy, from the dark sky.
In this whispered dusk, laughter will seep,
Wow, what a day, now it's time for sleep!

Twilight's Canvas

Brush strokes of orange splattered wide,
As night drags day on a wild ride.
The trees wear hats of deepening shade,
While frogs jump in, unafraid.

Fireflies flicker like tiny stars,
Making light with their buzzing bars.
The moon, a joker, beams through the leaves,
Hiding its chuckles behind the eaves.

A couple of clouds giggle and twist,
Creating shapes that no one could list.
"Is that a rabbit?" "No, just a shoe!"
"Nah, that's a taco! Just wait, it's true!"

As twilight paints with glittering glee,
Every critter feels oh so free.
This whimsical hour, so vibrant and loud,
Promises laughter, wrapping the crowd.

Shimmering Shadows

The sun dips low, a golden smile,
While squirrels play tag, all in style.
The sky turns pink, a painter's prank,
As birds all gather, their own little bank.

A dog walks by in a silly hat,
Chasing its tail, what a funny spat!
The breeze whispers jokes from the tree,
As butterflies laugh, so carefree.

Clouds roll by, like marshmallow fluff,
Tickling the sun, oh that's quite tough!
The world spins 'round, in a jolly dance,
While crickets start their own little romance.

As twilight sets, we giggle and cheer,
For the end of day brings laughter near.
With stars like twinkles in giant eyes,
We chuckle at clouds and their silly disguise.

Embracing the Coming Night

The day waves hello, takes a bow,
While shadow puppets dance, oh wow!
Crickets tune up their fiddles and bows,
As the moon peeks out, with a wink and a pose.

The neighbors' cat feigns a fierce fight,
With a leaf that flutters, a comical sight.
Fireflies start their glowing parade,
While frogs croak jokes beneath the shade.

Laughter echoes through the cooling air,
As kiddos run wild without a care.
The ice cream truck jingles its silly tune,
While night wraps the world in a warm cocoon.

As stars shine bright, we embrace the dark,
With shadows that play, they leave a mark.
So let's share a giggle, a laugh or two,
For nighttime brings joy, fresh and new.

Kaleidoscope of Dimming Hues

As colors swirl in a silly craze,
The sky wears a coat of sunlit rays.
A chubby raccoon steals a snack with glee,
While the sun winks down, how funny to see!

Giraffes in the distance munch on trees,
While hummingbirds giggle in the soft breeze.
The horizon blinks, in hues so absurd,
A painter has spilled his entire herd.

Frogs exchange jokes in a leaping contest,
While twilight arrives, in a quirky vest.
Colors pop out, in a vibrant spree,
Who knew the sky could act so carefree?

As laughter spills over from day into night,
The stars give a chuckle, all twinkly and bright.
With every shade, the fun never ceases,
In this wild dance, the heart never freezes.

The Solace of Evening

The day shrinks down like a playful cat,
While owls hoot softly, how about that?
With shadows that stretch and bow with grace,
The world takes a seat, in a cozy space.

Bats zoom by, in an aerial race,
With a flurry of wings, they slip and chase.
The breeze takes a tumble, giggling aloud,
As night wraps us in its warm, fuzzy shroud.

Neighbors gather 'round, their stories ignite,
With laughter and whispers, as day turns to night.
The stars join in, with a shimmer and gleam,
While the moon cracks a joke, or so it would seem.

So here's to the moments, silly and bright,
Where laughter abounds in the softening light.
As shadows deepen, and giggles take flight,
We find solace together in the warm, cozy night.

Brevity of Daylight

The day slips fast, like jelly on toast,
Fleeting laughter, like a shy little ghost.
Clouds wear socks, oh what a sight,
While the sun hides, just out of spite.

The birds complain, they can't find their hats,
Chasing shadows, like lazy cats.
They chirp and flurry, oh what a fuss,
Trying to perfect their evening bus.

The grill sizzles, burgers ablaze,
But soon they'll cool in the evening haze.
Fireflies dance, a twinkling parade,
As the sun sneaks out, no sunblock made.

Tick-tock, the clock does its jig,
Time's proposed, but can't do a swig.
So grab a laugh, before it gets dark,
For in jest, we find day's spark.

As Darkness Blooms

Night's a party, but no one's on the list,
As day retreats with a half-hearted twist.
The moon's a joker, playing peek-a-boo,
While the stars laugh loud, in their silver hue.

The cats run wild, in softening light,
Chasing shadows, it's quite the sight.
Crickets tune up, strumming their strings,
As the world spins low, like a barrel that sings.

Squirrels roll in, thinking it's playtime,
While owls just watch, with a hint of grime.
Pillows are ready for a cozy retreat,
But laughter's the bed, isn't life sweet?

With every tick, the world blinks twice,
Packing up hourglasses, oh so nice.
When darkness blooms, it's a slapstick show,
Comedy's crown—come join the glow.

Last Light's Serenade

A trumpet blares from the glowing sphere,
While shadows dance, no hint of fear.
The day's encore, a goofy charade,
Silly antics in the twilight parade.

Waves of laughter spill like spilled juice,
While the sun giggles, oh, what's the use?
Filling the sky with a wobbly grin,
It knows the night just can't help but spin.

The trees dance jazz, in a quirky pine sway,
As evening combs through in a quirky ballet.
Cacti are prancing in the cool breeze,
Shaking their spikes with whatever they please.

Life's just a stanza, a whimsical tune,
Echoes of chuckles beneath the moon.
So here's to the twilight, in all its delight,
Let's sing and dance 'til we lose sight!

The Glowing Farewell

A wink from the sky, the day's last kiss,
A cheeky wink, oh what bliss!
Silly clouds giggle, wearing gold crowns,
While the sun tiptoes, wearing clown gowns.

The trees chuckle, as branches sway,
Making room for the night to play.
Fireflies waltz in a comical spree,
Dancing around, for all to see.

The last beam of light, oh it takes a bow,
With a flick and a flair, it whispers, "Wow!"
The world erupts in laughter's embrace,
As night enters, with a grin on its face.

So here we stand, in the glow of the jest,
Embracing the quirk, life's heart in its chest.
When day meets night, always a show,
In this circus of light, on with the glow!

Farewell to Sol's Glint

The ball of fire sinks down slow,
As birds scream out their evening show.
The world gets dim, the sky turns red,
I think I left my pants in bed!

Chasing shadows as they flee,
I trip on rocks; oh woe is me!
A squirrel rolls by, it's quite a sight,
With acorn stash, it holds on tight.

The clouds are shaped like dinosaurs,
While goofy ants march out in droves.
I wave goodbye to blinding glare,
And wonder how I comb my hair!

With twilight here, it's time for fun,
A gameshow with the setting sun.
I toss my drink—it hits the sky,
And laughing stars all wink and sigh.

A Horizon of Dreams

When day gives up and night wakes up,
My dreams float by in a giant cup.
I try to catch them; they are fast,
And laugh at me—oh what a blast!

The light is fading, but who needs rules?
I dance like I'm wearing floppy shoes.
My shadow mimics every move,
In this twilight groove, I find my groove!

The trees wear hats of glowing gold,
And whisper secrets, brave and bold.
I joke with crickets, take a seat,
The night will bring us tasty treats!

With every star, a giggle shines,
Each twinkle tells of silly times.
So here's to dreams that never end,
And friends who steal your last donut, friend!

Chasing the Last Light

The sun tips its hat as it beams goodbye,
While I duck to dodge a flying pie.
The world's aglow in shades of fun,
I trip while trying to do the run!

A dog runs past, it looks quite hip,
With shades and swagger, it takes a dip.
The breeze whispers tales of mischief and cheer,
As dusk plays around—it's time for a beer!

I chase the last light with a hasty laugh,
While giggles explode like a funny giraffe.
In this playful dance with the fading day,
Lost shoes and jokes lead us astray.

And with a wink, the moon takes charge,
While goofy shadows loom quite large.
Time to grab a snack—oh, look at that!
A raccoon in shades thinks it's all a chat!

Elysium in the Evening

The evening wraps the day in bliss,
While I ponder why I look like this.
With snacks and drinks, the fun begins,
I swear those chips were smuggled twins!

As colors swirl like a silly dance,
The sky giggles at my failed romance.
I wave to stars, the shiniest crew,
Where aliens plot in neon hue.

I try to read the clouds above,
But they confuse me with their love.
A flying cat zips by my head,
Maybe it's time to go to bed?

Yet here I stand, a jester bright,
To prank the dusk with silly light.
In twilight's glow, I find delight,
Where laughter reigns, and dreams take flight!

Echoes of Day's End

The sun, it dips, what a sight,
A flaming orb, not ready for night.
Squirrels scatter, they race and flee,
Chasing shadows, oh, how silly they be!

Birds chirp loud, they sing their tune,
In the garden, a raucous raccoon.
He's looking for snacks to munch on tonight,
While the sky swirls in colors so bright.

A cat rolls over, all fur and fluff,
Chasing dreams, oh, he's quite tough.
A rabbit hops, with a wink and a grin,
As daylight fades; let the fun begin.

The stars peek out, making a scene,
While the moon is a giant jellybean.
As laughter echoes in the backyard space,
We cheer on the dusk, with a grin on our face.

A Symphony of Dusk

The horizon blushes, as if in shame,
A parrot squawks, calling a name.
Grasshoppers leap in a fiddler's dance,
While fireflies flicker, in their own romance.

Kids chase shadows, playing tag with the breeze,
An old dog snores, lying under the trees.
The air is filled with giggles and flair,
As puffs of clouds float like cotton in the air.

A sneaky raccoon steals all the fries,
While crickets serenade with their subtle cries.
Laughter erupts like popcorn in a pot,
As the evening's delight grows hotter than hot.

The evening's a show, with antics galore,
As folks gather 'round to laugh and explore.
With jokes and silliness under the twilight,
We embrace the madness, in pure delight.

Silhouettes Beneath the Dimming Sky

Shadows stretch in the evening's embrace,
While gophers wobble, quickening the pace.
A dog in a hat strikes a pose with a bark,
As the lawn chairs glimmer in the day's last spark.

Robins are dancing, what a peculiar sight,
Chasing their tails, all through the night.
With a toss of the frisbee, laughter unfolds,
As the stories of day become legends retold.

The stars start to giggle, or so they appear,
While fireflies waltz, creating good cheer.
An owl makes a joke, with a hoot and a wink,
As we gather together, we toast with a drink.

Under the twilight, our spirits climb high,
With grins that rival the moon in the sky.
As the curtain of night starts to gently drop,
We dance in the glow, we just can't stop!

Kaleidoscope of Evening's Charm

The light grows softer, what a wild hue,
As llamas graze, wearing shades just for you.
A goat photobombs with a cheeky bleat,
While kids spin 'round, in a rhythm so sweet.

The evening parade, oh, the neighbors all cheer,
As the raccoon brings snacks, drinks, and good cheer.
We laugh till it hurts, what a silly brigade,
Embracing the twilight in our grand escapade.

Fireworks of laughter burst in the air,
While a cat on a fence does a jig without care.
The air's filled with jokes, oh what a delight,
As we gather for tales in the glow of moonlight.

With giggles galore, and our spirits held high,
We share the bizarre, no reason to shy.
As the evening unfurls, with each cheeky charm,
We cherish this moment, a kaleidoscope calm.

Horizons Painted in Amber

As daylight hangs like a tired cat,
Dropping its paws on the sill of chat.
Colors spill like juice from a cup,
While birds squawk as they all hiccup.

A grandma shouts as she sweeps the floor,
"Hey, keep it down! We've got one encore!"
The clouds fluff up like cotton in fight,
Dancing around with sheer delight.

Kids giggle and point at shadows that chase,
Their laughter echoes, a raucous embrace.
While the daisies wear their golden tiaras,
In a field of laughter, as bright as a cinema.

But soon it's time for the crickets' call,
In this wacky ballet, we don't trip or fall.
For who knew dusk could wear such a grin,
As it cradles the day, letting night begin?

Starlit Promises Beyond

Tiny twinklers start to emerge,
Like winking gremlins with a humorous surge.
They giggle with glee in the dusky expanse,
Playing leapfrog with the moon in a dance.

A comet zips by, with a silly whoosh,
While owls are hooting, giving it a push.
The sky's a canvas, made of chalk,
Where dreams come out to do the moonwalk.

Even the planets join in the fray,
Juggling stardust in a cosmic relay.
They tumble and giggle, adding to the fun,
As laughter spills over, sights to stun.

With promises written in ethereal light,
They plan for tomorrow's goofy delight.
For who could resist a night such as this,
Filled with humor and celestial bliss?

Glistening Reflections of Night

Sparkly patterns start to appear,
As the water glimmers, giving a cheer.
Fish splash around with a comic flair,
Making the moon giggle as they dare.

While frogs in top hats recite silly prose,
With each splash they make, the laughter grows.
The water's like glass, but oh what a sight,
With ripples that ripple, in pure delight.

A raccoon wearing a crown of twigs,
Dances around while the dragonfly jigs.
The scene is complete with a cool twilight,
As laughter echoes into the night.

So come take a peek at this comic view,
Where night wears its giggles, all fresh and new.
For in these reflections, life's silly charms flow,
Beneath the twinkling stars' vibrant glow.

The Sigh of a Dimming Sun

As the day wraps up, in cozy retreat,
The sun lets out a sleepy, soft tweet.
With fingers of gold, it waves goodbye,
Sending shadows upon the earth to lie.

Oh the sun's got jokes, as it cools its blaze,
Poking fun at clouds in a lazy daze.
It twirls and dips in a grand pirouette,
While the world below chuckles in duet.

Even the mountains can't stay serious,
With silhouettes that look quite delirious.
The trees sway and laugh, in gentle hum,
As the day whispers, "It's time to come."

So gather 'round friends, as day takes a bow,
For the laughs of the sun are upon us now.
With each little giggle, as bright as the tin,
Life's just a comedy, where we all fit in.

Farewell to the Fiery Orb

The orb begins to take a dive,
Waving goodbye, it's quite alive.
It's off to paint a nighty scene,
Leaving us with shades of green.

The sky blushes in shades of red,
Like it's wearing a fancy thread.
Clouds giggle in the fading light,
As day takes off and bids goodnight.

With a wink and a cheerful grin,
The fiery one lets the fun begin.
Stars pop out like little dots,
Ready to play and tie up knots.

So pack your bags, it's time to roam,
The orb has called it a day at home.
As night takes over with a cheer,
We'll dance 'til dawn and shed a tear.

Echoes of Daylight

The day's last giggles start to fade,
As shadows dance in a prancing parade.
Little crickets tune their tiny tracks,
While daylight's fun takes a break to relax.

The sun beams down a final tease,
But even it can't escape the breeze.
The sky erupts in colors bright,
Time to say 'goodbye' to blinding light!

Like a clown at a carnival show,
It flips and flops, oh so slow.
The echoes linger, a funny sound,
As laughter spins and spins around.

So raise a glass to the day that was,
Let's make some memories, just because!
With a chuckle and a playful sigh,
We wave 'til night comes sneaking by.

The Edge of Night

At the edge of day, where giggles play,
The sun takes a bow, waving, "No way!"
It plops down low, like a tired clown,
As hues of pink start parading town.

Frogs croak out their evening tunes,
The stars come out, sporting cartoon spoons.
Each one ready for a splendid spree,
Bringing laughter for you and me.

As night descends with its sprightly scarf,
It gathers giggles, ready to laugh.
The hush of day can't steal the fun,
In this playful dance, we've all just won.

So let's twirl 'neath the coming dark,
With dreams so bright, we'll make our mark.
We'll blow kisses to the fading light,
Embracing joy, oh what a sight!

Above the Dusk

High above where shadows play,
The sun gives night a grand ballet.
With pirouettes and a blazing wink,
It sends the clouds on the brink.

Silly stars peek through the shroud,
Waving hello, feeling proud.
A stellar party's in the air,
They twinkle, and jive without a care.

As dusk throws hues across the skies,
We cup our ears to evening's sighs.
For jokes are tossed like seeds to the night,
In this cosmic play, oh what a sight!

So join the laughter, take a seat,
The universe dances to a funky beat.
Above the dusk, where giggles reign,
Let's ride the stars like a comet's train!

Stars Awaken

As evening yawns with a sleepy grin,
The stars stretch wide, they're here to win.
They pop out bright, in a twinkly show,
Making sure that night's no woe.

One by one, they start to laugh,
And take the stage, what a fun craft!
With sparkles shooting around like jelly,
The universe feels a bit more merry.

From puddles of light to whispers of blue,
They roast the day like a marshmallow stew.
So giggle and dance in the night's embrace,
As stars play tag in their cozy space.

So here's to the stars, those jolly sprites,
With stories they share on magical nights.
Let's toast to the sparkle, the laughter, the fun,
As the playful journey has only begun.

Creatures of the Dusk

As the day slips away, cats start to prance,
Chasing shadows that lead them to dance.
A dog joins the fray, a bounce in his bark,
Squirrels hide nuts, the daylight's gone dark.

Frogs croak a tune in their slimy attire,
While crickets chirp loud, a nighttime choir.
Fireflies zip by, like lights on a spree,
'They can't catch us now!' — a shout from a bee.

The raccoon's got snacks, hoarding like a pro,
He glances around, 'Is it cool to show?'
The owl gives a wink, adjusting his glasses,
Says, 'Enough with the drama, just watch all the masses!'

Creatures of dusk, a silly parade,
Living their lives, not a moment delayed.
They giggle and snicker, and join in the fun,
Perhaps to return when the next day's begun.

A Tincture of Night

As colors dissolve, watch a painter at work,
The sky takes a dip, just ask the old stork.
The clouds wear their pajamas, fluffy and bright,
While the moon peeks out, all ready for night.

A squirrel in a top hat, stealing the scene,
Plans his grand heist with his buddy raccoon.
'No trees to climb now!' the chipmunk does tease,
They chuckle and wiggle, a real comedy spree.

The bats have a meeting, but can't find a seat,
They say, 'Next time we'll meet on the edge of the street.'

The stars all look down, wondering aloud,
'Is being a formation still trendy or proud?'

And just as they settle, they hear their cue,
A firefly bursts forth, 'Hey guys, I'm brand new!'
They laugh and they wobble, welcoming change,
In this tincture of night, it's never too strange.

Echoes of Evening

The sun takes a bow, a dramatic retreat,
With a wink to the earth, it puts on its seat.
The shadows start playing, holding their breath,
Squirrels gossip low about daylight's death.

A llama looks up, adjusting its cap,
'These twilight outfits? They're really a trap!'
The stars giggle softly, twinkling with glee,
'The night makes no sense, but we love the spree!'

With a flip of a tail, the fox starts a game,
Chasing the whispers of rocks with no name.
The owls hoot advice, but nobody hears,
They laugh till the night's filled with all of their cheers.

The echoes ring out, a bizarre lullaby,
As creatures of night wave the daylight goodbye.
In this playful chaos, the cosmos aligns,
With memories locked in, as joy intertwines.

The Fading Ember

A cozy old bonfire flickers and fades,
While the last few sparks twist like clumsy parades.
Marshmallows are roasted, too charred for delight,
'It's a brand new flavor!' shouts one in the night.

The crickets all chuckle, finding it absurd,
While a raccoon sneaks in, trying to steal their bird.
Hot dogs roll away, escaping the heat,
'Come back!' yells a grill, 'Don't you miss my sweet beat?'

Ghost stories take flight as the moon cracks a grin,
While the stars all sit back, letting laughter begin.
The embers grow dim, whispering goodbyes,
It's a show of the night under swirling dark skies.

Yet the fire remains, now a glowing quilt,
Of memories cherished, of laughter built.
And as we sit back, the fun never ends,
In the fading of embers, the warmth always blends.

Twilight's Final Breath

The day wears a coat of bright orange,
As the sun hides behind the sea's fringe.
Clouds giggle in hues of fuchsia and pink,
While the crabs on the shore start to wink.

The seagulls recount jokes in the air,
As the world dances without a care.
Breezes whisper secrets to trees,
And the light says, 'Chill, I'm just not pleased!'

As shadows grow long and stretch like a cat,
Even the fish claim this land, imagine that!
They leap with delight, making waves that chime,
And the sun says, "I'll be back, just give me some time!"

So raise a glass to this playful jest,
For the day's end is simply the best.
A nap for the sun, a show for the night,
And the stars peek out, ready for flight.

Colors that Breathe

Orange peels scatter across the sky,
As the sun winks, saying goodbye.
The purple jiggles, the blue takes a bow,
While the clouds make faces, 'Look at me now!'

The horizon giggles, a canvas so wide,
While the sky splashes hues, and the day takes a ride.
Little birds chirp, 'What a splendid sight!'
As they prance homeward, hearts feeling light.

The breeze feels like laughter, tickles and plays,
As the creatures prepare for a crisp, starry phase.
Even the flowers lean in and peek,
At the showcased colors, vibrant, unique.

So we paint our dreams with this swirling delight,
Color our memories, and embrace the night.
For tomorrow will return with the same joyful scream,
In a world that's alive with a colorful dream.

The Surrender of the Sun

The sun bows down, with flair and style,
"Catch you later!" it says with a smile.
A medley of shades, a twirl and a twist,
As the sky throws a party, it can't be missed!

The clouds wear hats, all fluffy and bright,
While the stars whisper, "We'll shine later tonight!"
Crickets start cracking jokes on the ground,
As the sun gives a wink, then glides out of town.

Mountains chuckle, casting long, silly shadows,
While the water reflects this playful bravado.
Laughing leaves tumble in the soft breeze,
While day bids farewell with the greatest of ease.

So here we are, waiting for dark,
Ready for tales by the moonlight's spark.
But let's not forget this comical spree,
For every end is a new jubilee!

Evening's Palette

The paintbrush of dusk stirs thoughts in a way,
That even the grumpy old sun wants to play.
With strokes of gold, and a dash of divine,
Even the critters gather for wine.

Birds take a bow, then twirl in the air,
While bugs take their seats, like they're at a fair.
"Look at that orange!" whispers a leaf,
As it brightens the branches, shedding the grief.

The clouds wear shades, reflecting each glance,
As the shadows begin their evening dance.
Everything giggles, the moon gets ready,
While the stars laugh and hold their confetti.

So join in the fun, the spectacle thrives,
As nature builds dreams where laughter derives.
For dusk's gentle art, in joy does extend,
Painting moments that never quite end.

When Daylight Bows

The sun dips low, a grand farewell,
With clouds as dancers, do they rebel?
Shadows stretch, they play a game,
While crickets whisper, calling your name.

A squirrel in shades, adjusts his tie,
With acorns as riches, he aims for the sky.
The day shrinks back, but we don't despair,
We'll roast marshmallows without a care.

Fireflies pop out, like tiny sparks,
In a blurry race, they leave their marks.
As daylight kneels in an awkward bend,
We laugh at time, our funny friend.

So raise a glass to the fading light,
With goofy grins, we embrace the night.
The world spins round, with silly tunes,
As moonbeams join the carefree goons.

Horizon's Melancholic Serenade

An orange blob, it melts away,
While geese waddle in their ballet.
The world sighs, a comedic puff,
As critters question, 'Is this enough?'

Waves clap their hands, so very loud,
While surfers tumble, feeling proud.
A wise old tree, grins from its spot,
Saying, 'Next time, don't try my knot!'

The clouds wear hats, slightly askew,
Murmuring secrets, just us few.
But light's a prankster, it plays and hides,
As winks of twilight, o'er us resides.

So grab your jester cap, let's convene,
For nightfall's not as grim as it seems.
In shadows, we find, in laughter we twine,
A melody sweet, a comedy divine.

Chasing the Last Rays

With ice cream cones, we run like fools,
Chasing bright colors in handy tools.
The sunlight giggles as we trip,
But we bounce back, ready to flip.

Dogs join in, with wagging tails,
In a parade that never fails.
Sing out loud, a silly refrain,
The sun's a prankster, but who complains?

A wild banana flies through the air,
"Is this how fruit takes to the fair?"
While kids build castles of dough and sand,
The horizon gives a cheeky hand.

So here's to whimsy that never dies,
As we dance beneath the painted skies.
With laughter echoing, bright and clear,
Time fades away, but the joy is near.

The Stillness Before Night

The world slows down, a lazy yawn,
As colors fade, a comedic dawn.
Stars peek out from their cozy nap,
While owls giggle in a nighttime slap.

A teddy bear, in a moonlit frame,
Holds a dance party, all the same.
Lamps flicker with a winking glare,
As if to say, "We're still aware!"

Cats plot mischief, with a twinkle in eye,
As shadows whisper, "Let's give it a try!"
The dusk takes a breath, all is still,
As chaos waits at the night's thrill.

So gather close, let's share a laugh,
As darkness paints a goofy path.
For in this moment, all is right,
Before we dive in, the fun of night.

Evening's Gentle Farewell

The sky's a canvas, painted bright,
With giggles of clouds taking flight.
A flamingo flies with a silly grin,
Waving goodbye to the day it's been.

Squirrels in shades wear hats so neat,
Sneak a peek at the sun's retreat.
They spill their nuts with glee and cheer,
As twilight nears, we hold 'em dear.

The stars come out, all twinkling bold,
Like little lights, brave and cold.
They laugh at us as we trip and fall,
While chasing shadows, oh what a brawl!

With fireflies waltzing around the field,
And laughter echoing, forever sealed.
The day waves goodbye with a wink and smile,
As night comes knocking in style.

Radiance Weaves Goodbye

A cat in shades lounges near the door,
While sunbeams play on the kitchen floor.
With jellybeans tucked into its paws,
It yells, 'Time for naptime, because!'

Mountains blush with hues so wild,
As crayons forget they were ever filed.
A giraffe is painting with style and grace,
While llamas join in the evening race.

Yo-yos swing in the fading light,
As ducks with glasses take off in flight.
They quack a tune, oh what a sight,
Making us snicker with pure delight.

The moon rolls in like a disco ball,
Casting shadows big and small.
Stars toss confetti, oh what a show,
As the day waves bye, taking a bow.

Shadows Stretch Beneath the Sky

As shadows stretch on the grass below,
A potato starts to dance and glow.
It twirls and spins, with no care to hide,
While the sun chuckles, all puffy-eyed.

A squirrel drops ice cream, what a fuss,
As it slips and slides, oh what a plus!
The clouds giggle, puffing in glee,
All joining in on the slapstick spree.

Time ticks on, but we can't worry,
As llamas in shorts start to scurry.
The horizon blushes in shades of fun,
While stars pop out, one by one.

So, hold your giggles, don't let them flee,
As we welcome night with unbounded spree.
The moon takes a bow, a curtain call,
Ending the day for one and all!

Colors Dance on the Edge

Colors pirouette just like they're high,
As the sky giggles with a twinkling eye.
Balloons take flight in every hue,
Chasing the day that once flew true.

With every blush, a joke unfolds,
As pumpkins dance in their orange and golds.
The sun tosses rays with a playful glint,
While a chicken hatches a comedic stint.

Mice wear boots, and they feel so spry,
Popping and locking, oh me, oh my!
Fireflies join for a flash mob cheer,
As giggles erupt, ringing in our ear.

So wave that curtain on this day so bright,
As the colors meld into the night.
With laughter as our guiding star,
We bid adieu, wherever we are.

The Gilded Hour

A golden glow, a sight so fine,
The cats start claiming their throne divine.
The dog, confused, begins to prance,
While shadows stretch and stars start to dance.

With lemonade mustaches, we cheer and grin,
As ice cream drips down, where do I begin?
The sun slips down, wearing shades so cool,
While we toast marshmallows, aren't we a fool?

A squirrel steals cookies, calls it a feast,
While birds hold a meeting, a chirpy beast.
Laughter paints the sky in colors so bright,
As twilight giggles and steals our delight.

Where the Sky Kisses the Sea

The seagulls squawk, what a racket they make,
As sand slips between toes, a funny mistake.
We build castles that look like a mess,
While the tide sneaks up, with minimal stress.

The waves whisper jokes, so salty and sweet,
The breeze tugs at hats, what a flip-flop feat!
A crab scuttles past, with a strut and a show,
While dolphins high-five, performing a glow.

Beach balls soar high, like balloons of delight,
As laughter echoes, in soft fading light.
It's a splash, a giggle, a day full of fun,
Where the waves say goodbye, and the laughter's not done.

A Tapestry of Fading Colors

Painted skies in shades that tease,
We giggle as our hair blows in the breeze.
The crayons fell out, a colorful mess,
Who put blue on the cat? I must confess!

With watermelon slices, we munch and cheer,
As ants hold a banquet, our picnic they steer.
A friend drops their drink, what a funny sight,
The ice cubes jump, as they take flight!

The clouds wear pajamas, fluffy and light,
While we swap our stories, a silly delight.
With each laugh echoing, our voices take wing,
In this fading spectrum, joy's what we bring.

The Last Flicker of Radiance

As the day waves bye with a wink and a nod,
We dance like we're silly, the twilight's our pod.
The fireflies gather, like stars with a glow,
While we chase around, wanting to show!

The bugs throw a party, they say, "Join the fun!"
But we swat with wild arms, oh what have we done!
A laugh that erupts, like popcorn in heat,
As we trip over sneakers, oh how we compete!

The last flicker mocks, with a tease and a grin,
As night rolls in softly, we can't help but spin.
With dreams now igniting, we sleep with a tale,
Of all the chuckles that danced on the trail.

www.ingramcontent.com/pod-product-compliance
Lightning Source LLC
Chambersburg PA
CBHW072220070526
44585CB00015B/1422